Prompt: How to get started with writing a Career Journal

52 Prompts for setting up and writing your Career Journal

www.printedportal.com/prompt

Copyright © Printed Portal
All rights reserved. No part of this document may be shared or reproduced without written consent of Printed Portal.
ISBN 978-1-291-83353-9

Introduction

Whatever your project, your job, your business - whatever YOU want to be using your time for - WE are here to help and support you.

Whatever it is that you want to do and you hear yourself say "I just haven't got the time". STOP!

Remember everyone has the same amount of time - the same number of hours in each day. Think about what others have achieved - your potential is the same. With the right strategy and mind-set - This WILL be you.

The good news is that you have taken that first step in the right direction. Thank you for purchasing this product.

This book is here to help you set up and use your own Career Journal so you can get a head start with your Career and Personal Development.

We believe that you will find tremendous value in the information contained within this book and that the prompts (and weekly actions available on the website) will serve you well. Please take the time to go through the exercises when setting up your Career Journal – you might just be surprised about what you discover about yourself and your career along the way.

You **NEED** this book if you:

- are looking to find some direction and start setting goals.

- are looking to actively manage your career development.

- are a professional looking to stand-out from the crowd and not just manage but **maximise** your career development.

- are looking for a new job.

- are looking to advance your career.

- want to create a record of your professional life.

- want to learn from your mistakes and the mistakes of others.

- want to plan your future.

- **Want to unlock your own Career Development potential and take control.**

So let's get started.

Chapter 1: Why, What, When and How?

> **Career Journal Prompt #1:**
>
> **Read Chapter 1 and complete the end of chapter checklist.**

Why use a Career Journal?

There are so many arguments for using a Career Journal and so many advantages yet Career Journalists appear to be a minority and journal in secret without much direction or focus. This changes today!

We are not saying you announce to your employer that you are a Career Journalist, but we are saying that you make a firm commitment to yourself and to your career that you are going to give it some TLC over the next year (and beyond) by keeping a Career Journal. This will include taking positive actions for the benefit of your career and most importantly dedicating some time to nurture your career.

Ask yourself this question: At the moment how much time do you dedicate each day or each week to Career Planning and Development? If you are like the majority of us your answer probably is "not much at all". In fact you probably don't even dedicate time on a weekly basis or even a monthly basis to your career development. This changes today!

Whatever your circumstances a Career Journal is a positive, focused and dedicated way to take control of your career development. A Career Journal will help you discover things about yourself, about your chosen career, about your workplace and help you plan for the future. It can even help you look for jobs, prepare for interview and get that promotion you are after.

Whatever your aspirations a Career Journal can help you get there.

Using a Career Journal allows you a set amount of time to dedicate to THINKING about your career development without worrying about other things. During this dedicated time you can then think, write and reflect about things like your current situation, potential ideas and career planning.

These are of course specific reasons for using a Career Journal, but all the benefits of regular journaling still apply to your Career Journal – including improving physical and mental health, developing your writing and communication skills and using it as a personal growth tool.

What is a Career Journal?

No two Career Journals will be the same, but they should all have one thing in common - they are a collection. A collection:

- of dreams;
- of thoughts, feelings and emotions;
- of frustrations;
- of goals and aspirations;
- of achievements; and
- of soul and passion.

A Career Journal is a tool for managing and recording your career development. What it should include will depend on why YOU need your Career Journal and what you are going to be using it for.

So let's start by working out why YOU need a Career Journal. Which one of the following statements best apply to your current circumstances:

- You have a vision of the perfect job but don't know how to achieve it and you are looking to find some direction.

- You are stuck-in-a-rut or missed out on a promotion and are looking to actively manage your career development.

- You are a professional looking to stand-out from the crowd and maximise your career development.

- You are looking for a new job.

- You are thinking about a career change but don't know what you want to do or how to get started.

- You are a student or recent graduate starting out.
- You want to go self-employed.

A Career Journal can be used in all these circumstances (and in all circumstances that we have not specifically listed). The important thing is that you realise that a Career Journal can help and we can help you find a starting point.

What you include in your Career Journal will depend on your current circumstances and what you want to achieve. However there are a few keys elements that should be common to all journals such as those listed below:

- free writing journal entries;
- an analysis of your current situation and a job history;
- career goals;
- daily or weekly career planning objectives and actions;
- a record of career related achievements and progress;
- writing and polishing your Career Tool-Kit and other materials and correspondence;
- job interview questions and answers;
- salary and job research; and
- a training record.

Some extra elements should be included depending on your goals and objectives.

Even if you are a seasoned career professional a Career Journal can simply be a place to record and document your professional life and you can use it to:

- Process information;
- Document information;
- Monitor daily work habits;
- Learn things about how you work;

- Debrief after a particularly challenging or simply long term project; and
- Record positive feedback and learning points.

Simply put: a Career Journal can help everyone.

When should you use your Career Journal?

You should use your Career Journal when you want to focus on your career development and advancement.

The easiest way to find time for your career development is to schedule it in. How often you work on your career development and how much time you dedicate to your Career Journal, prompts and action plans will depend on your current situation and what you hope to achieve.

- For an active job-seeker looking for a job should be your full time job and therefore your journal should complement this.

- For someone looking for a new job or career change while in a full time job should be dedicating an hour a day or 5-7 hours a week minimum.

- A student should aim to be somewhere in between the two.

- For everyone who is just managing their professional career development to improve their chances of a promotion in the future or someone who is not actively looking for a new job but keeping their eye on the market a couple of hours a week should be sufficient.

So once you have decided how much time you want to dedicate to your career development – book in a basic but regular time slot into your schedule. You can of course be flexible but it is useful to have a regular appointment in there.

Finally, we shouldn't need to remind you of the basic rule that career development should be something that you do in your personal time and your Career Journal should be kept safe at home. There will, of course, be a few prompts and actions that you can do on company time, in your lunch break and/or and using company resources for example company appraisals.

If you are required to keep a career development or training reports or record for work purposes we suggest that you complete these in a separate notebook or word document so that they are not mixed up.

Your Career Journal is a personal thing.

How should you keep your Career Journal?

If you already keep a personal journal you could add your Career Journal into your existing routine.

At the most basic level a Career Journal can simply be a journal with a 'Career Development Focus' listing and exploring things such as ideas, quotes, job descriptions, articles from magazines, memories, wish lists, interesting things you have read online. Using it as you would for any other aspect of your life.

However, we believe that a Career Journal is a specialised project and needs that something extra, something special and something empowering which is why we started creating these prompt products.

There is no right or wrong way to document or record your Career Journal entries. You just need to make sure you:
- choose a method which will ensure that you regularly make entries in your journal;
- enables you to do the exercises and prompts; and
- allows you to do an efficient review of your journal.

Choose a medium you enjoy. Type it, write it, paint it, draw it. The options are endless.

Here are some examples of different ways to document your journal:
- Notebooks;
- Filofax, Planner or Binder System;
- One Note;
- Workbook; or
- Sketchbook.

What will you choose? Make your choice today.

Chapter 1 Checklist:

1. What is the main goal of my Career Journal?

   ....
   ....
   ....
   ....
   ....
   ....
   ....
   ....
   ....

2. How should I document my Career Journal entries?

   ....
   ....
   ....
   ....
   ....
   ....
   ....
   ....

3. What is my motivation for keeping a Career Journal?

   ....
   ....
   ....
   ....
   ....
   ....
   ....
   ....
   ....

Chapter 2: Motivation, Inspiration and Goals

Motivation and Inspiration

Writing a journal (any journal) requires motivation and discipline. A strong motivator will in time develop or change your journaling into a habit. Once it becomes a habit and an enjoyable routine the more useful and beneficial the journaling exercises will be.

In Chapter 1 we threw in a sneaky question into the checklist asking "what is your motivation for keeping a Career Journal – a motivator can give you focus and a sense of purpose above and beyond the prompts, actions and even your end goal.

> **Career Journal Prompt #2:**
>
> **Write your first freehand journal entry using the topic of "Motivation, Inspiration and Goals" and at minimum answer the considerations listed.**

<u>Journaling Considerations:</u>

1. What is your motivation for writing a Career Journal?
2. What is your motivation for achieving your end goals and any other career-related goals that you have?
3. What de-motivates you?
4. How can you boost your motivation?
5. What inspires you to be better at your job?
6. Write down THREE motivational or inspiring quotes in your Career Journal.

Journaling should never be a chore but there will be times when it feels like you have nothing to contribute, nothing to write or need that extra kick. However, there are a number of things that you can use to boost your natural motivation:

You may wish to consider:

- getting support from friends and family;
- finding a buddy;
- using action steps and tracking your progress;
- sticking your career development plan on the wall (literally);
- learning to being proactive instead of reactive;
- generating excitement by visualising your success;
- overcoming disruptions and disappointment before you get started;
- taking part in the Career Development Prompt Series at www.DIYCareerdevelopment.co.uk;
- Putting a reward based motivational system in place.

So why have we asked about motivation in the first place? This is because we want your Career Journaling to become a habit and part of your regular routine. We have tried to get this started by scheduling time to work on career development and write in your Career Journal and these shall be backed up by your motivation to achieve your Career Journal Goals.

You know the generally accepted rule – 30 days to change or create a habit. So while we don't expect the majority of you to commit to writing a daily Career Journal starting the habit of writing daily for the first 30 days of your Career Journal can help you to catch up on the backlog of information that should really already be in your Career Journal (and make writing on a weekly basis easier).

Career Journal Prompt #3:

Accept the Challenge!

30 Days to Create a Career Journaling Habit

☐ **I ACCEPT**

Your Career Journal Goals

A Career Journal can be a great way to declare, track and reward yourself for achieving your goals. However, making your Career Development Journal Plan requires an understanding of what makes you work well and motivates you to ensure that you keep on track for achieving those goals.

Everyone should have a list of the following goals:
1. "Things I want to achieve in a year"
2. "Things I want to achieve in the next 5 years"
3. "Skills and Training Goals"
4. "Career Journal Goals".

However, in this chapter we want to focus on your Career Journal Goals. You have already declared the main goal that you are going to use your Career Journal for.

For the purpose of this example we shall use the end goal of BEING PROMOTED. In the Chapter 1 Checklist you will have written something like "I am going to use my Career Journal to get myself a promotion this year".

That is great! You have made this first step. Now you have to write a Career Development Journal Plan and set out your Career Journal Goals to help you get this promotion. An example would be:

GOAL 1: Set up my Career Journal.
GOAL 2: Write a Career Journal entry each week.
GOAL 3: Schedule 5 hours of career development time per week.
GOAL 4: Do the "30 days to create a career journaling habit challenge".
GOAL 5: Use my Career Journal to update my C.V.
GOAL 6: Use my Career Journal to record my achievements.
GOAL 7: Use my Career Journal to do salary research.
GOAL 8: Use my Career Journal to prepare for my appraisal and promotion interview.

The first few are general goals that would be suitable for everyone; the next few are specific goals to outline HOW you are going to use the Career Journal to obtain your main goal.

Career Journal Prompt #4:

Write your Career Journal Goals

If you are still not sure about what you need to do to achieve your goal just decide on the goals set out in the goals list on the next page.

My Career Journal Goals

GOAL 1: Set up my Career Journal.

GOAL 2: Write a Career Journal entry daily/weekly/monthly/anytime.

GOAL 3: Schedule ……………. hours for career development every day/week/month.

GOAL 4 : Do the 30 days challenge.

GOAL 5: Write my Career Journal Goals and Career Development Journal Plan.

GOAL 6: …………………………………………………………….

GOAL 7: …………………………………………………………….

GOAL 8: …………………………………………………………….

GOAL 9: …………………………………………………………….

GOAL 10: …………………………………………………………….

Chapter 3: Write your Career Development Journal Plan and design your Career Journal Set-Up

Finalise your Career Journal Goals and Career Development Journal Plan

So to recap on what we said before let's clarify why YOU need a Career Journal and what you hope to use the Career Journal to achieve.

Remind yourself which one of the following statements best applies to your current circumstances:

- You have a vision of the perfect job but don't know how to achieve it and you are looking to find some direction.

- You are stuck-in-a-rut or missed out on a promotion and are looking to actively manage your career development.

- You are a professional looking to stand-out from the crowd and maximise your career development.

- You are looking for a new job.

- You are thinking about a career change but don't know what you want to do or how to get started.

- You are a student or recent graduate starting out.

- You want to go self-employed.

This is your starting point for writing your Career Development Journal Plan. This book is an introduction to Career Journaling and therefore does not include a dedicated plan for each of these scenarios but we have included a few small examples of what each type of Career Journalist might include and more information will continue to be posted on the website.

Career Journalist: Career Developer

- Career Path Analysis
- Promotion and Pay Rise Plans
- Preparation for Appraisals and Performance Reviews
- Marketing and Inter-Company Networking
- Training

Career Journalist: Job-Seeker

- Job Market Trends
- Training and Personal Development
- C.V. and Application Polishing
- Volunteering
- Job and Job Applications Tracking / Review
- Interview Preparation and Review
- Dream Jobs / Wish List
- Recruitment Agencies

Career Journalist: Career-Changer

- Career Research
- Work Experience
- Transferable Skills
- Further Education / Training

Career Journalist: Students

- Education and Exam Results Record
- Internships/Work Experience
- Graduate Scheme Research
- Career Path Research
- Job Applications
- Dream Jobs/ Wish list
- Job Market Research and Trends
- Contact and Networking

Don't worry you don't have to set out step by step what you are going to do – but what you should be thinking about is what elements you need to include in your Career Journal so you can maximise its potential with your specific goal(s) in mind.

Career Journal Prompt #5:

Finalise your Career Development Journal Plan based on getting from your current situation to where you want to be.

Setting up your Career Journal

Now that you have written your goals and your Career Development Journal Plan it is now time to set up your Career Journal so that you can start using it straightaway. In chapter 1 we included different ways you could document your journal and at the end of chapter 1 you made a decision about how you are going to document it.

For the task of setting up your Career Journal you will now need to combine the medium with the goals and plan set out in this chapter.

Set-up Example: Notebook as a Career Journal

If you are sticking to the basic Career Journal and simply free-writing your journal there is very little set-up required. Simply find a suitable notebook and start writing. A notebook is great for a daily or weekly entry style journal, but is less efficient for using the prompts, projects and Skill Development Plans.

What makes a good notebook for your Career Journal?

- Cover: Quite often people go for a more business-like journal for their Career Journal, but this does not have to be the case. One of your criteria can be a visually fun notebook (both for the cover and for the paper). We give you permission.

- Size: When making a decision about size you should consider where are you going to be using your Career Journal? Career Journals can range from A6 through to A4 in size and some people even use larger sketchbooks.

- Paper: Most people go for lined notebooks, but you can use plain, squared, mixed and even illustrated – think about the types of notebooks you enjoy writing in. The more you enjoy it and better it feels, the longer you will write.

- Organisation: Unfortunately, the downside of a notebook is that you cannot usually reorganise and categorise the pages. For example you might wish to keep your job history in one section and your interview questions and prep in another section. If you do use a paper notebook and want a little bit more organisation than general free-writing you might wish to go for a repositionable notebook instead.

Set-Up Example: Filofax, Planner and Binder Systems as a Career Journal

Using a Filofax or binder system gives you more flexibility than a notebook as you can redo, add and reposition pages. This makes it easier to write and file your prompts, projects and Skill Development Plans.

Our e-products are designed with paper-based systems in mind and can be easily printed in A4 or A5 size and placed in your binder or

Filofax. Of course you can always write out the prompts and activities on any paper of your choice or alternatively use our own workbooks.

Having a binder rather than a notebook also allows you to organise (or reorganise) your papers depending on your goal or objective. For example your own set up will change when your circumstances change, so when you change from career progression to opportunity hunting or from job-seeker to starting a new job or even from a university student to a graduate whatever your transition may be the ability to modify your binder and your set up can be a huge advantage as you can recycle your material. (Of course, there is nothing wrong with simply starting a new notebook or workbook as you will inevitably run out of space whatever medium your choose.)

Set up your binder or Filofax by deciding what elements you want to include and create dividers for each of them.

Set-Up Example: One Note as a Career Journal

For those of you who wish to document your Career Journal electronically but don't want to simply use Microsoft Word or another word processor a great option is frequently overlooked Microsoft One Note. This allows you to create an electronic notebook for your Career Journal and set up tabs and pages and organise and reposition your content as you wish. It is also great for creating to-do lists and clipping articles and information from the internet.

Simply create a new workbook and label the sections at the top with the different elements of your Career Journal and within each section you can then create your pages and subpages for your content. Pages can be moved, deleted, copied, and filed, providing you with the ultimate flexibility.

Set-up Example: Workbook as a Career Journal

For those of you wanting stricter guidance on what you should be writing (and when) the Workbook edition provides this structure. You can either print off the e-copy or order your own colourful print copy of the workbook. The workbook requires no set up and is designed for you to write in as you please. Starting NOW! Visit our website for more details.

Set-Up Example: Sketchbook as a Career Journal

If you are more artistically minded or enjoy smash-booking buy a special dedicated sketchbook or a suitable crafty notebook and draw, sketch, paint and collage your way to a fun and creative Career Journal. You could even document it using photographs.

Now that you have your tools let's get started.

Career Journal Prompt #6:

Start your Brand New Career Journal. Do anything, just start!

Chapter 4: Building up the Back Story (AKA the "30 Days to create a Career Journaling Habit Challenge")

Last chapter you accepted the challenge of creating a Career Journaling Habit in 30 days by journaling daily. You might think "I am not going to have anything to write", or you might simply think "I am crazy" but the rationale behind it is really quite simple:

Firstly, we want to help you create a journaling habit, after doing it daily for 30 days you will have no problem doing it on a weekly basis or even continuing to do it daily.

Secondly, it helps you build up the content of your Career Journal, your reference material and your back-story so that it is a useful resource from the word "go". By participating in this challenge you will successfully pull together the information to make your Career Journal a useful resource.

So let's get started.

DAY 1	**Career Journal Prompt #7: Review your career goals for the last year**
- What goals did you have in the last year? - What goals did you achieve? - How did you accomplish these goals? - What goals did you miss out on? Why?	
Completed:	

DAY 2	**Career Journal Prompt #8: What did you achieve in the last year?**
- What did you achieve in the last year? - What can you learn from your successes? - What can you learn from your failures? - What makes your achievements ACHIEVEMENTS?	
Completed:	

DAY 3	**Career Journal Prompt #9: Set your Goals for this Year**
- What are your Goals for this year? - Write out the actual steps to be taken. Clear. Actionable. Steps.	
Completed:	

DAY 4	**Career Journal Prompt #10: Write a Description of your Dream Job**
Include in detail everything that you would use to describe your dream job.	
Completed:	

DAY 5	**Career Journal Prompt #11: Write a list of the Top 10 Companies you would like to work for**
- What are your top ten companies to work for? - Why?	
Completed:	

DAY 6-16	**Career Journal Prompt #12-22: Research one of your top 10 each day and find out what you would need to do to get a job there!**
- What roles would be suitable for you? - What qualifications, extra skills or training would you need? - Check current vacancies - Check the recruitment process - Make notes	
Completed:	

DAY 17	**Career Journal Prompt #23: Add a copy of your latest C.V. to your Journal**
Locate a copy of your C.V. and add it to your journal. A full review of your C.V. will be carried out at a later date. If you have any older copies of your C.V. – include them for comparison	
Completed:	

DAY 18	**Career Journal Prompt #24: Write a list of all the things you did in work today – a snapshot**
You can chose to either do a detailed 'day in the life' style entry or simply write a list.	
Completed:	

DAY 19	**Career Journal Prompt #25: Write about your Education History**
This should include your schools and university (if any), the years you attended, the subjects you studied, your individual grades, your overall grade, extra credit activities and any other information you can remember.	
Completed:	

DAY 20	**Career Journal Prompt #26: Write out an overview of your Job History**
At the most basic level this should be dates, employer, job title as a timeline.	
Completed:	

DAY 21-23	**Career Journal Prompt #27-29: Complete a Job history review of your last three jobs**
(or all of your previous jobs over a period of three days). Write about what jobs you did, your responsibilities, dates and contact details.	
Completed:	

DAY 24	**Career Journal Prompt #30: Write a list of your Computer, IT and Technical Skills**
Include specific software and programs where applicable.	
Completed:	

DAY 25	**Career Journal Prompt #31: Write a list of your Job Specific Skills**
Think about what you do day to day and think about what would be on the job description as essential and desirable skills for your job.	
Completed:	

DAY 26	**Career Journal Prompt #32: Write a list of your Soft Skills**
Soft Skills or Transferable Skills are those skills you have gained simply by working in an environment that develops those skills e.g. communications skills.	
Completed:	

DAY 27	**Career Journal Prompt #33: Write a list of the Training you have done in the last year**
Include training courses and events that you have attended in the last year.	
Completed:	

DAY 28	**Career Journal Prompt #34: Write a list of ALL the Training you have done**
Simply write down all the training courses you can remember doing. You can exclude those you wrote down yesterday.	
Completed:	

DAY 29	**Career Journal Prompt #35: Write a list of all the things you did in work today – a snapshot**
You can chose to either do a detailed 'day in the life' style entry or simply write a list. (Yes, we are doing this again).	
Completed:	

DAY 30	**Career Journal Prompt #36: Where do you want to be in 5 years?**
Think about what you want to achieve in the next five years	
Completed:	

Chapter 5: What should I be writing?

Now that you have completed the 30 day challenge you should be ready to ease into your normal Career Journal routine. As a Career Journalist you will firstly be using your Career Journal as a record of your professional life. This is what your free-writing section of your Career Journal is for.

There is no limit in what you can put in your free-writing journal – this is up to you. Our suggestions include:

- achievements and celebrations;
- learning points;
- interesting conversations;
- Career inspired thoughts;
- inspiration and motivation;
- networking events and opportunities;
- lists;
- articles you have read; and
- your reading lists

Career Journal Prompt #37:

Use your Journal to Keep a Record and Write!

Perhaps the most important prompt in this book. You should be using your Career Journal (either through free-writing or prompts) to keep a record of your job and your career development.

Far too often we don't think about what we do in our day to day job – we gloss over things that seem irrelevant and only really consider what we do when we find ourselves in a job-hunting situation.

This is where keeping a Career Journal comes in.

It allows you to keep a record of your job in more detail than you may normally remember. This information can be used towards:

- appraisals
- promotions and pay rises
- writing and updating your C.V. and
- nailing an interview for a new job.

(to name a few).

The prompts will help you address specific issues and turn them into actions, but keeping a free-writing journal and keeping a record on a weekly basis of your current job can be an amazing resource of information. So if you haven't done so already – schedule in 30 minutes a week for free-writing and reflection. If you already keep another journal you can of course incorporate your Career Journal entries into your existing routine without too much hassle.

Chapter 6: Using a Career Journal to Achieve your Goals

Secondly, journaling can help you with particular career development orientated objectives and we include in this book some brief guidance on:

- Using a Career Journal to prepare your C.V.
- Using a Career Journal to record your Goals and Career Aspirations.
- Using a Career Journal to write a Skill Development and Training Plan.
- Using a Career Journal to help ask for a Pay Rise or Promotion.
- Using a Career Journal to nail that Job Interview.

However, there is just so much that can be said about all of these objectives, so we have chosen to only cover the main points to get you started.

Using your Career Journal to prepare your C.V. and completing your Job History Records

One of the most essential items in your Career Tool-Kit is your C.V. If you are looking for a job or get offered an opportunity (which can happen completely out of the blue) you will want to have a good C.V. prepared. So regardless of whether you are actively looking for jobs you should try and maintain an up to date C.V.

However, having an up to date C.V. is not only great to have in case a job opportunity arises but it also helps with tracking your development - we learn a lot about ourselves by knowing **how** we got somewhere and what tools we used to do it. Learning **how** you have developed over the years can help you build up a comprehensive job history and help you identify which C.V. (if you use multiple CVs or styles) was the winner.

If you are not actively looking for a new job you should still refresh and review your C.V. every 6 months. If you are actively applying for jobs you should be tailoring your C.V. to each application you make.

Career Journal Prompt #38:

In prompt #23 you dug out a copy of your C.V. – now it is time to review it

---

1. **Carry out a review of your current C.V.**

What prompted you previously to write a new version or revise your CV and how often do you do it? If you are anything like the majority of us it will have been when you were last looking for a job. If it was the C.V. you used to get your current job is it going to be very outdated and really not useful in its current state.

2. **Note absent C.V. worthy achievements**

Even if your C.V. is not going out to anyone, those recent C.V. worthy achievements should still be noted for two key reasons:

- On the off-chance that someone asks for a updated copy of your C.V. you can quickly refer to your list and update the CV as necessary.
- So that achievements are not overlooked when sending out your next job-hunting C.V.

Create a Master C.V. which records everything. It does not matter if it is very long. It is way too early to be picking and choosing achievements and skills as you have absolutely no idea what will be included in the job description of the next job you will be applying for. Any of your achievements might directly relate to experience that they are looking for.

If you cut down your list of achievements and experience too early, you might simply have glossed over and forgotten something that could be key to your next job. It might even be the difference between getting an interview and not. So record everything on a master C.V. or on a list in your Career Journal.

3. **Update your C.V.**

The next part of this action plan is to actually update your C.V. even if you think nothing has changed since your last update - you might be surprised.

If you are already completing your journal entries and exercises this may be even easier than you think. If you are not already doing journal entries, complete what you can and schedule a second review in 3 months rather than 6 months.

Updating your C.V. should include the following:

- your current job, skills and responsibilities;
- changes since your last CV e.g. internal promotion;
- key responsibilities;
- key achievements;
- training;

> **Career Journal Prompt #39:**
>
> **Tidying up your timeline and accounting for any gaps in your Job History**

During the 30 day challenge a number of the prompts were geared at jump-starting your job history section. At the start of your job history section you should include your timeline and then a detailed section on each of your previous jobs.

In reality your C.V. should only include relevant jobs and may not account for all gaps in your job history. The job history section of your Career Journal saves you the effort of remembering all this extra information that you may need one day.

Include everything in your job history section starting with your school years (no matter how long ago they were) no one is going to see this information – it is for your benefit. Your safety net.

Take a closer look at any periods of unemployment. If there are any current or recent gaps for example in the last 3 years in your job history write a paragraph explaining the gap and note how you spent your time. For any period of travel, maternity leave or career breaks which you may not consider a period of unemployment or gap – make sure you include it in your personal timeline.

Refer back to your current C.V. and check if there are any gaps in it that you should be filling out. If it is not possible to account for them on your CV but you think that they may be picked up upon. Prepare an answer for being questioned about the gap at interview.

> **Career Journal Prompt #40:**
>
> **Complete a Job History Review for each of your previous jobs.**

If you took part in our 30 day challenge you should have already completed a Job History Review for your last three jobs. These records should ensure that you have a comprehensive and factual account of your previous employers as well as generate some insights into your time there.

Now it is time to do a review for **all** your previous jobs and you must make sure that you complete as much information as you can. It is also useful if you have the time to do a check on your previous employer to see if they are still called by the same company name and if your reference contact still works there. It can be useful to note any name or personnel changes in your review.

As well as the factual account you should be carrying out an 'end of job debrief' in your Career Journal, especially for recent job changes. This should address questions like why did you leave? What did you learn? For more historic jobs this can be difficult, and if you do not feel that they can be completed only complete the factual review.

If you are a job-seeker and looking to change jobs you should also complete an 'end of job debrief' for your current job to help assess your feelings about the job and put you on the right footing to answer difficult questions about why you want to leave your current job at interview.

Using a Career Journal to record your Goals and Career Aspirations

What are you? If you haven't already defined yourself – do it now!

- What are you? What do you want to be?
- What are your next steps?
- What are your intentions?
- What are your employer's intentions?

Career Journal Prompt #41:

If you don't know your Employer's intentions for you – schedule THAT conversation with your boss and come away with strong and clear action points to follow.

Sometimes goals can be about balancing your own goals with your employer's goals and expectations so let's review and see where they match up and where they differ.

It is also important to know what is needed to get things signed off – far too often decisions about your career and your future will be made by people who do not know you and have never met you. This can be disheartening if you are not successful, so prepare by knowing what is needed. A properly laid plan taking in your employer's needs can improve your chances of meeting your goals.

Career Journal Prompt #42:

Write your Career Goals List

Write your goals list or revise your Career Development Goals Notebook to plan your goals.

Career Journal Prompt #43:

Write your 5 Year Plan

In one of the previous prompts you were asked the question where do you want to be in 5 years? Now it is time to draw up a five year plan. This should be more than a list of things that you want to do over the next five years. Instead it should set out a rough time frame for the things that you want to achieve during these next five years.

When writing a five year plan you should consider including:

- deadlines (all and any);
- conferences and events;
- submission dates for awards, competitions, and articles;
- project details and deadlines;
- appraisals and opportunities; and
- working abroad/ travel.

Everything and anything – just stick it on there.

Using a Career Journal to write a skills development and training plan

A Career Journal can be used to help you write and follow a Skills Development Plan and a training plan. Ideally you should have both a Skills Development Plan and a training plan. A Skills Development Plan covers actions that you are going to do to develop a particular skill. For example, if you have decided that you want to develop your communication skills and you might commit yourself to writing an article for the website, or giving a presentation, but you would not necessarily need to do a training course in communication skills to do this. A training plan covers courses and formal company training that you attend – such as safety and industry updates and continuing professional development. (There can of course be an element of overlap.) As a Career Journalist you should be proactive about keeping a record of your plans and tracking your progress.

> ### Career Journal Prompt #44:
> ### Carry out an Initial Skills Analysis

There are multiple occasions where a skills analysis should be carried out:

1. As part of your Career Journal Set Up.
2. Prior to writing your Skills Development Plans
3. When reviewing job descriptions and reviewing job applications.

Yes, that is right. You should do separate skills analysis each time you make a job application. By recording this in your Career Journal it can help keep a record, and allow you to track your progress and review your Skills Development Plan at the same time. So let's start and carry out an initial skills analysis now.

Start by reviewing your Skills. Skills come into two categories:

- Skills I have; and
- Skills to Improve.

When reviewing your skills try and split them into these two categories. What skills do you already have? Try and write these down on the "Skills I have List". Consider separately the skills you want to improve on or think you need for your ideal job. Write these down on the second list.

Now let's review the "Skills to Improve List" and consider whether the skills to improve are the same skills you need for the jobs you are applying for (if you are a job-seeker), the role you want to attain (if you a looking for a promotion) or simply your dream job or opportunity.

When reviewing the "requirements" on job descriptions split them into the same two categories. Only this time evidence the skills you do have and note which skills you need but do not have or do not have the required competency.

Finally consider HOW you are going to improve or obtain these skills and whether you have the means and resources to improve and develop them.

It might be as simple as taking on an extra project at work, attending a course or you may just need to push a little further on something you are already doing at work to match or reach the desired competency needed.

This will be the start of your Skill Development Plan - add an action to your to-do list for the HOW you are going to obtain the skills you need to improve. Then actively work through the list of skills to improve.

Career Journal Prompt #45:

Write a Skills Development Review and Plan for each skill you want to develop

For each Skill Development Plan you should answer the following questions:
- What is the skill and what is expected of someone with this skill set?
- When have you used this skill to date and what is your current level of competency or experience?
- What opportunities have you had to demonstrate this skill? (Both inside and outside of the workplace).
- For each opportunity - write about your experience in full and then note the 'highlights' that would be put on your CV or that you would mention in interview.
- What is missing that you need? Are you current examples enough?
- Review your C.V. - what on your C.V. currently demonstrates your skills? Do you have a better example? Can you get a better or stronger example?
- How can you improve your skill set and obtain the competency required?

Career Journal Prompt #46:

In prompt #33 and #34 you jotted down your initial thoughts about your training to date. Now let's work out if you need a training plan and write it!

There are a number of courses readily available in our modern world whether these are run by professional bodies, dedicated companies, local universities, other local organisations or online.

Courses (whether they are required by your job or not) are a great way of expanding your skills, knowledge and adding something to your C.V. They are equally important regardless of whether you are a job-seeker, looking for a promotion or looking for a career change.

For most people they will simply need a simple training record to record their on-the-job training but don't be afraid to trying to achieve something more (while still maintaining your training record).

Training should feature as part of your career development plan. It should also be considered in your five year plan and when preparing for your appraisal.

Also, if work won't provide you with the training or you want to learn new skills outside of your job description are you prepared to find the time to sit the course and fund it yourself? Yes? Are you intending to go above and beyond your employer's expectations? Yes? Then you need a training plan.

Before writing your training plan write down your answers to the following questions:

- What training have you already undertaken to get here?
- What training are you required to do by law or company policy?
- What training does your employer provide you with?
- Is there any else they should be providing you with?
- Is there anything you already do online / in your free time?
- What training do you need for get the job/position you want?
- Will your employer provide you with this training?
- What form will this training take?
- Is there anything else you need to do yourself? How?
- What is next?

Once you know the answers to these questions you can start to think about coming up with a plan.

Using a Career Journal to help you nail that interview

There are a number of ways you can gear your Career Journal towards preparing for and mastering an interview including interview preparation and evaluating each interview.

Interview Preparation

An interview is not an exam. People can very easily fall into the trap of treating an interview (and preparation for said interview) a bit like an exam.

- By cramming
- By leaving preparation to the last minute (night before or the train journey) and
- By "winging it"

It is important to appreciate that an interview for a job requires preparation. It is not a simple matter of reaching into the dark recesses of your brain for a nugget of information that was mentioned at a workshop six months ago. There will be new things to learn about in advance. At minimum this is usually the background about the company you are interviewing with.

A Career Journal can help you manage and focus your interview preparation for each job as well as create a bank of resources for interview preparation dedicated to your personal career path.

> **Career Journal Prompt #47:**
>
> **Regardless of whether you're a job seeker or not – pick one of those job interview questions that always throws you or that you always stumble on. Now write the draft answer. Review it 3 more times at different intervals.**

The Post-Interview Review

Interviews whether they are successful interviews or not are learning experience and provide the opportunity to learn more about yourself, about different interview processes and learn more about the company you are interviewing with.

> **Career Journal Prompt #48:**
>
> **Review and evaluate each interview**

Don't be scared of doing more interviews, getting more practice and fully analysing and evaluating each interview your have.

Using a Career Journal to help ask for a pay rise or promotion

There are a number of ways you can gear your Career Journal towards preparing to ask for a pay rise or a promotion. We have included some examples below to get you started.

Keep a record of your achievements

You should be keeping a record of your achievements anyway. But if you are looking to impress your employer and/or justify a promotion or pay rise you will also have to keep a record of your achievements in 'their language' which is usually in terms of money, sales, client wins, profits etc.

So:

- Identify what you would need to show to justify a pay rise or promotion
- Determine how you can evidence this and keep a record.

Achievements in themselves may not be enough so it is also important to ask (or identify) what is NECESSARY for a promotion (if you haven't already).

Create a Step by Step Plan

At a time when money is tight, employers are not always willing to hand over a pay rise or promotion based your sales figures alone. Your boss might not even have the authority to give you a pay rise or promotion – so do your research to find out what is needed and record this research in your Career Journal.

Career Journal Prompt #49:

Write an Action Plan based on your Research

If there is no set career path or obvious role for you to progress into, why not take the initiative and style your own job.

Career Journal Prompt #50:

Write your own job description

Even if there is a set career path write your own job description anyway and see how they compare. When you come to taking the role refer back and see what could be negotiated or incorporated into your promotion package.

Prepare for your Appraisal

In its most basic form an appraisal is a performance review. It might be directly tied to a promotion or a pay rise and in many companies it is the only opportunity for you to brag about what it is that you do and for your boss to realise what it is you actually do for the business.

Appraisals (whether they are annual or otherwise) are an important way of monitoring your progress and are usually your official and possibly only means of recording and communicating your efforts. So no matter how nervous you are or how much you hate appraisals make sure you prepare, put your best foot forward and make them count.

Your Career Journal can help you prepare. Start by noting the deadline for completing your appraisal review and schedule a meeting with your supervisor in advance. (Make sure these dates are in your diary.)

Prepare for the appraisal by reviewing your notes from your previous appraisal and complete the appraisal form in advance of your meeting. (Don't forget to proof-read and review). If it is your first appraisal review the sample form or an example from a colleague who is willing to share.

Before the meeting make sure you know what you want to get out of your appraisal and consider both your objectives and your company's objectives - equally.

Your Career Journal can help you with these preparations and you should keep previous appraisals and notes about those appraisals in your Career Journal as well.

Learn from Feedback

Appraisals are an important way to obtain feedback from your employer so make sure you keep track of what is being said and then after the appraisal meeting:

- Review what you wanted to get out of your appraisal meeting and make sure you got it all. If not, follow up after the meeting.
- Review what was agreed at the meeting and note how this can help with your overall career development objectives.
- Follow up any outcomes and actions points as soon as you can. If they can't be done straightaway diarise them.
- Use it to work on your professional relationship with your boss.
- Make sure you get your appraisal form signed off and submitted.

By following these steps you can ensure that you maximised your appraisal meeting.

Of course appraisals are not the only type of feedback you get and all feedback (good and bad) should be worthy of a note in your Career Journal as a learning experience in respect of the bad feedback and as positive reinforcement in respect of the good.

It is also handy to keep a record/copy of positive written feedback as well.

Career Journal Prompt #51:

Dig out your most recent Appraisal Form to review – Are you meeting the objections and goals that you agreed with your employer. Is your employer doing everything that they said they would to assist you.

> **Career Journal Prompt #52:**
>
> **Finally subscribe to our mailing list and the blog at www.DIYcareerdevelopment.co.uk for weekly prompts**

Congratulations! You did it! You have set up your Career Journal and are well on your way to making Career Journaling a habit. Now you are ready to create your dreams and make real progress with your Career Development.